MIRRAN THOUGHT

MIRRAN THOUGHT

Spitzwiesenstr. 50
90765 Fürth
Germany

www.dwmirran.de
www.empty.de
empty@empty.de

READ FOURTEEN (MT-592)

ISBN 978-3-7386-5013-6

Printed by BOD - Books on Demand
In de Tarpen 42
D-22848 Norderstedt
www.bod.de
info@bod.de

First printing 2015

MIRRAN THOUGHT is the publishing arm of Mirran Threat, a company devoted to releasing the music and writings of the various members of Doc Wör Mirran. Mirran Thought and Mirran Threat are both divisions of MT Undertainment.

Red Pepper, Blue

Joseph B. Raimond

Written 2013 to 2015 in Fürth,
Germany

As always, in loving memory of Frank
Abendroth.

For Conny, my perfect angel

Dedicated to Neal Cassady

Cover art by Joseph B. Raimond
"My Love" watercolor on paper 2003
Fürth, Germany,

This is DWM release Nr. 129

Betting on a Losing Horse

Little boys, so blind to the
Evil of a mother, play outside
Football and hide and seek

Ready to hide from their future tyrants
Boss, bitch and boobs,

> Boobs, that jelly from above
> But only when one is lucky

Boobs will tie a man down with their
Sheer weight, and he won't mind
At least at first
But when he finally does, fuck!
It's too late, asshole!

Tyrants:
Often an all-in-one package,
And at a bargain price!
Always vying for control of his poor soul

And so the story continues,
and when the ball and chain
Was finally cut, it lay open to the elements

The tear drenched rain slowly rusting
Away the links that had once
So enslaved his very happiness

And the ball lay open
For all to see, to laugh at and to mock
And the ball felt foolish, for it was naked
And all could see the cracks, the faults
It was not perfect after all

It lay exposed to the eyes of those
It once tried to control

But that fine feeling,
Drunk on power, the rage that set
Him to trembling......was.....

Gone!

        Shit!

Seeing that fear and hatred radiating
From his blue eyes, the ball felt fear
For the first time, of being alone,
Of being without power,
Of being without fuel to power that hatred
Of being left with nothing

The ball never forgot, and ever since
Has been trying to regain than glory
Like the fallen dictator dreams from his
Plush South American residence
The ball longs for the days of power
When blues eyes jumped at the word
When nagging was taken seriously

But for all it was, it was never love
Disguised as it was at the beginning
Fooling everyone, even blue eyes
Love it could never be

It was the black side of life, frozen
Night forever, with no chance of dawn
No warmth, no light
No sun and no tenderness

A spiritual black hole, sucking
Sucking in all that was positive
Until the darkness would be complete
Until deprivation would be complete

Hell,
Plain and simple

And since it was hell,
What do you think that makes you?

No, it is only the light that matters
In these precious few seconds we are given
And you have already wasted most of mine

What? Forgiveness?
Forget forgiveness,
How can a simple being forgive something
So evil

Feeling so small, meaningless
There is no space left for forgiveness

I am like your sculpture
Always being chipped away
Chipped away, smaller and smaller
Until nothing
Not even a core, an essence
Is left to live

Perhaps nothingness
Is pure male perfection
(in the eyes of a female)

Blood and tears,
There is always something flowing,
Blood, tears, blood, tears
I am so sick of these rivers
Oceans

It is time to freeze
For in a frozen world
Blood and tears cannot flow

So, now you know
Why I don't like to jump into cold water
Although I did learn to swim

And so the days pass, and the experiences mount
Finally coming into line with the average
A few dreams get fulfilled along the way
And a few nice memories vie for space
Among the many bad

It is time to stay positive, live for now
All the while
Romanticizing about the "good old days"
The number of which seem to be increasing
With each day!

Even one or two with you as the main star

But don't flatter yourself
As you're usually naked, and middle aged

While living for the now
My face grows wrinkled and weary
Weary of you, while still craving

I sit and play with my trains
Paint out of vanity, for myself
Write and jam

But you are always there in the back of my mind

Ready to pounce, like the predator you are
Destroy me, destroy the little I have built
Drag it through the dirt of your insults
Take off the shine I have worked so hard
To polish

You are all a sickness, combined
And alone, a virus,
Some harmless, others deadly

And your particular disease is
Negativity, gloom and doom
All is shit, everything is worthless
And you are never at fault of all that
Misery around you, that so flows
Through you, like the heart you are
Feeding your disease to all those around you
For we are all miserable, deathly
Ill

We look it
We feel it
We know it deep down in our souls

As we struggle with our spiritual health
In the face of your onslaught of hate
We are brothers in poverty
Brothers in deprivation
Brothers in need and
Brothers in misery

Misery loves company

But you:

Eaten by hate, pure, cannibalistic
It feeds you, you feed it
Your hate grows
     Grows
          Grows
               Grows
                    Grows

Until in overwhelms all that is around you
The virus is healthy on hate, larger than life
Immune to happiness and cure

Your hate is so relentlessly hungry
You are feeding on your own life
Sucking at your own life's blood
Just make sure that pain, is somewhere

I will let my inner light shine
And I know, like in my very soul
That my spirit is strong, when restless

And that it can conquer a simple virus

Mother nature is so good
At making points
That stick you, that sting you
That make you think

A front, battle lines are drawn
We have dug into the trenches
Will face the winter with frozen
Tears and blood
And we will be numb to pain

And through the fighting, the danger
I will continue to dream
A dream of a beautiful
Perfect angel
That will come to rescue me

She will be perfect

And will love me forever

Come back to reality, now, boy!
There is a time for dreaming
And a time for fighting

The virus has gathered its forces
Is charging the front
Casualties are mounting
Blood is flowing
Screams can be heard
Death is in the air
Bombs are exploding all around
Gunfire, explosions, gunfire!

What, did you really think this would be easy?
You've been through it before
It was your decision
And you knew what was coming

But our fight is good, our fight is right
And victory will be ours!
Good will triumph over evil
Let god sort 'em out!
The virus will be eradicated!

Just hold on a little longer!

Defeat
Cannot, will not, be considered
It is not an option

All little boys become warriors
They play their little games
Cops and robbers
Cowboys and Indians
You be the good guy, I'll be the bad guy

Training, getting ready
For real life, the reality of war
That we all know, all too well
And from which we can never escape

And it is the war that kills us,
No, not the loneliness
Not even the broken heart

It is the regret that poisons us
And kills us,

In the end

That is why, I cry
When I see my little boy
Playing his typical little boy games

For he is so pure
So full of life and love
And I know that in the end
He will lose the war like all the fathers before
In all the generations before

And there aint a damn thing I can do about it

It is the unborn that are lucky
For they will never have to fight
They will never have to lose love
They will never feel the sharp sting
Of regret

They will never have to look at themselves
In the cruel mirror
And watch their bodies grow old
And haggard

They will never have to put in the effort
Just to exist

They will never have to put in the monumental
Effort, needed
Just to crack a smile now and

Then

For every virus
There is a disease
And your disease, has grown
Growing, growing, overtaking me

Psychological pain is now giving way
To pure physical pain
As gut starts rotting, and I sit here shitting
Buckets of blood

And each disgusting drop
Has your face mirrored on it.

But here, behold, the perfect medium
To paint your portrait
Over and over again!
Each more perfect than the last
Pure inspiration!

But I am getting closer to solving the puzzle
And each little clue, brings me closer
To conquering you

Your face = pain =
Ball and chain = death =
The black void = nothing

So, you win, even in death

But
Don't think I give up so easily

Pen to paper is one of our most potent weapons
In this perpetual war
And so I will write, write and write
          Write, write and write

A literary diplomat, if you will
In this world of wars

Just get me off the battlefield
I have enough scars for a lifetime
Lucky to even be alive

Yes,
Yesterday might be gone forever,
Forever out of reach,

But the scars remain, and they still hurt
And they will coin the future,
          The hope,
The hope, if there even is any left

Strange, I looked in a mirror, too
But I didn't see a cloud, only a lonely face
Nothing unclear there
Nothing hard to define or hard to understand
But maybe hard to accept

And maybe you are right,
I do still want to fuck you

But that isn't my scared mind talking
But the fucking biological programming
I don't know how to turn off

For the unflattering truth on this side
Of the Atlantic is,

Like a computer, I cannot tell if you are beautiful
Or not
My biology programs me to want you
Not for your mind, but only for your body
Nothing but a physical process
Could be anyone, just as long as
She's got a hole

What do you find attractive in that?????

??????

Do you feel better now?

I thought I was a caterpillar
Destined to one day change from ugly, land bound
To flying high in the sky, and so pretty
But no, that was not to be me
I am a worm, squirming,
In a blind panic, all I can do is feed and shit
And I don't see what or who it is
Trying to feed on me
So ask me a question and watch me squirm

I'm not as elastic
As bubblegum
And I don't taste as good
There is just so much
You can pull on me
Before I fall apart

My heart is skipping beats
As I return to you, again
And again
And again

Accept me as I am
Open your arms,
   Your heart
      Your legs

I shouldn't be asking, I know
It is against the rules
Of our peace talks, our treaties
Our demarcation zone
Our contracts and your agreements

But loneliness can't be defined
Nor controlled
By your contracts

As a desperate being, my list of things
That I shouldn't do include:

I shouldn't dwell on yesterday
I shouldn't worry about tomorrow
I shouldn't eat so much fat
I shouldn't drive so fast
I shouldn't drink so much
I shouldn't…..
I shouldn't be thinking of you
I shouldn't be falling in love with you

The shadow, although horror
Is still home, like
A prison is still called home by the inmate

The shadow that stalks, also offers comfort
For it is the unknown that we truly fear

I do not want to find out
What happens when we die

You do it, and just let me know what it's like

Maybe I'm not a worm either
But a slug, slimy and slow
Only good for causing disgust
In the eyes of the pretty
Only good for ruining your garden
Only good for nothing

Whatever I am, it is deformed
It is weak and you don't want to look
You say you can't see it,
But I know it is there

If only I could have been a bird
I'd fly so high,
Bathe my colorful feathers in the sun
No wonder birds sing in happiness all day

And,
I'd shit on the heads of people I didn't like

Puckered lips, and pseudo love
Couldn't hide your cruelty´
You devoured what little love I could
Muster
You thrashed and slashed at my fragile
Temperament, until it hung like ripped rags
In the cold wind of your heart
Until I froze through, not a bit
Of warmth remaining
Old bones, for an old day
Never to sleep, never to separate
The soul from the body
All fused together in ice
Chip away, it doesn't matter
You will not find an essence
Of anything but gloom

Dirty ice chips will litter the floor
Dirty slush like on the side of a downtown
Corner after the snow has begun to melt

Frozen gloom

A crippled heart

So many hands, all ripping and chipping
All wanting their little piece of me
Then they fight for the little pieces of gloom
Like the train station pigeons
As they fight and rip
Apart the remains
Of a fast food hamburger

So take what you want
I have learned long ago that resistance
Brings only more pain

And when you have your little piece of my gloom
You will then see
It will never be enough

I feel blue but I see red
Fire rips through my heart
Shooting out as laser beam hatred
My gaze boring deep gashes in your tyranny

I am a dragon

Mustering my strength for the battle
But doomed to extinction and legend
When I am dead, and all those than knew me
It will be as if I never existed
And that is the true horror of life

I try so damned hard
To live for this moment
Maybe if I could just once
I would finally feel a bit of happiness

My gloom like trading cards
Collect them all!
Trade with your friends, build your collection
Only while supplies last!

I need a breather, time out to rest
To collect my thoughts, look around
Take stock and get ready

But it is hard to take a rest
When you are always trying to catch up
With your happiness

And run away from
Your gloom

The gloom
Is like a black hole, sucking in everything
Absolute darkness, total despair
Where light never shines

Like its own dimension
A smile is never real, cannot exist
All color is black,
Form becomes formless, fluid
All music is white noise
And poetry is meaningless words

Including all that poetry
That I once wrote for you

Meaningless
Nothingness

Go away

All I ever wanted
Was someone at my side
Pretty, intelligent
                Sexy
                        Equal

Who would look at me with love
In her eyes

All I ever got were conflicts, nagging
                    jealousy
                                   hostility

And someone who looked at me with
Indifference

Gagging at the thought of your voice
As it dug into my guts, slashing
My self-respect, my self confidence
You were out for my blood
Wanted to see the pain in my eyes

I
Too weak to fight back

Whisky bottles litter the floor
Testify to my battles

Our
We
Always ended up being only
Your
You

Humping, always humping
As you all traded me, back and forth
Strap on another face, doesn't matter which
Maybe a few different sizes of tits

And you always claimed it was love
Humping was never love

Gagging on the words
You demanded to hear
They stuck in my throat, gurgled
And ugly
Finally said, I knew in my bones
They were always a lie

And always that humping!

Raping someone's innocence into
Formless hatred, good work!
Another one ruined, destined for the couch
Analyzing away those hours
Trying to make sense
Where did it all start, what did I do wrong?
Fighting with the accusation
I deserved it all along

Pain can occupy so many dimensions
And defy the laws of physics

Plummet to man
Your talk of life
Only meant my death
Plummet to man

I smell risk
I am bleeding, but I don't know where from
Somewhere, something is hurting
But I can't find the pain
Why are you standing so close to me
But you never touch me, teasing
You smell of sex, but your partner stays faceless
A faceless, nameless man, or perhaps woman?
It doesn't matter when it is always someone else
Who gets to fumble your breasts
Always behind locked doors, our fancy
Our imagination runs wild, torturing us
With images of your copulation
Over and over,
Always with someone else
Never with me

Never,
            Ever

I am walking, no plodding
Towards something, anything?

Violent thoughts accompany me
Revenge is a dish
Best served with hot sauce

I see the shame in your eyes
When I confront your violence
You know it was wrong, don't you?

So stop telling me I deserved
What you dished out

Evil dreaming, you dream of me
As a thing
You control, manipulate
      Fuck
            Suck
                 Rape

Evil dreaming, night torture
Playing games, teasing
Pretending it is love

It was never
Ever
Love

I am like a river
Always there, but always different
Flowing, creative
But you were a dam
Blocking my life, away

I am like the sky
Everywhere at once, but often blue
But you were smog
Choking life away with your filth

I am like the good earth
Mother Nature's son, rich in life
Offering nourishment to the world
But you were my erosion
Ugly, industrial landscaping
With no heart, no spirit

I am like fire
I can give you warmth, I can also burn you
And I can be damn hot!
But you were the fire department
Dousing my flames with your cold words
And the ice in your heart

The elements were my father, my mother
They created me in love
You destroyed me in hate

So many years lost
In a stillborn marriage
They didn't live happily ever after
And the bad guy was not killed

Reality was a bad part two
A sequel that no one wanted to see

Dragging the ball and chain
Through this world
I still seek comfort
     Happiness
     Love

The ball and chain slowed me down
For sure
But I have never given up

Your cruelty has become part of me
Like a leech, it sucks at my spirit
Like the virus that you are
You make me sick

I vomit at the thought of your face
I cough at the smell of your sex
I shit at the thought of your custom
I bruise at the thought of your touch
I bleed at the thought of your violence

And,
I still look for a miracle drug, my cure
A potion that will set me free
Of disease, of you

I will fly, free of pain
Soar the sunny, warm skies of happiness

And sing songs of the birds,
Of freedom

As you whither below in your dark cesspool
Clutching at me over your head
The hate in your eyes glowing red in the night

Finally, I am out of reach

Sometimes

I find a word, and it decides to reside
In my mind

Sometimes

I welcome the word, sometimes not
But in this guest, I am reminded of you
Some aspect of you

Sometimes

I fight the memories, want to banish them
To unwritten history
But the word has other plans
And makes me face the white page

Sometimes

The resulting art is good, even great, maybe
Sometimes not

Sometimes

The art is pretty, usually not
But it is real, and that is what matters most

Just how did you catch me?
With tainted flattery to my ego
Stupider than any fish
I went for the bait, was caught in your net
Never noticed you coming in for the kill
As I swam around your pretty tank
Boy toy play thing

But when I decided to aspire
Find my humanity, confront my weaknesses
You were quick to reveal my inferiority
Fed my insecurity, all the while
Trying to squash my dreams
Aspirations were to you my trash
Get real, come down to earth
Don't try to be something you cannot be

Wallow
Another nice word
The pig that I am, I wallow
In my dirt, my filth
My porn and my perversions

I am a man, after all

But my dreck is open and honest
For all to see

You are the real perversion
As you can hide your deformities, ugliness
Weaknesses and violence
Behind a pretty face, nice tits
And legs spread open

You are the real perversion

Suffer, the word

You suffer arrogance
I suffer at your violence
We both offer nihilism
It is all we ever had in common

I stay invisible to the happy
It is what I prefer
It is what I know as reality

Better to hate what is real
Than to love a lie
Learn to be content in misery
For that is all that life really offers

Emotionally slaughtered
Like a bleeding goat on an unknown god's altar
I lay, helpless
Having given you my secrets, my fears
You turn on me, hurl my hurt back at me

Your words: helpless, weak and lazy
But infinitely sharp
Cut into me, worse than my bones you broke

When it was too late to go back, you sit
Pretending to cry, or trying maybe
Doesn't matter

No salted tears flow
Frozen in your arctic heart they stay
Forever locked away, for no man to see
Never to feel, flow, tasted by a true love

They might as well not exist

Now, a new chapter begins
Before the previous has ended
Chapters all blur together
In a haze of promises, sex
Lies and disappointments

The words become meaningless
As they are repeated over and over
The stories told are by heart
As they are repeated over and over
The smiles are forced,
As they are repeated over and over
The interest is forced
As it is repeated, over and over

All right, come on over, let's get it over with

I am doomed to play the games
To perform, to pretend interest
To go shopping and listen to your gossip

But just when, when
Will one of you take the time
To look for, however long it may take
To find the long lost key
That can open this lonely heart
All I ever wanted was a moment of happiness
As I skate around the edges of insanity and grief

The forever black
Always pulling me, down

All I ever wanted was an anchor
To prevent me from falling

A Sunny Day

A sunny day, and I feel better
For a brief moment, you leave my mind
And I can think clearly
And I can act normally
And soak these tired old bones
In the care of the mother sun

Will I now be able to paint my rainbow
In color, and not always in black?

When we force happiness upon
Ourselves, we despair and doubt
But it is never a mistake

So sad, your departure
The light of your smile
Was a gift to the world around you, to me
As it warmed my heart
For a brief, fleeting moment

For we have hearts
For falling in love
Not for breaking

And never for hating

This is not Hollywood
This is reality
Real love is holding your hand
Taking care of you when you are down
Growing old together
Facing death together

A life, readying in departure
As another lies, in waiting
The circle of our lives
Centered on our ideal of love

Finally, just let me love you

Breathing is heavy
As you lash at my back, scratching
Proof of a good lover,
Boast, show my friends

But the real scars are on my heart
Safely hidden away
Where no one can see
I finally fled, in fear for my life

Into the unknown (to me)
World of ecstasy, empathy
Finally apathy and boredom
As lovers lined up
All with their sagging breasts and fat thighs
Fighting for a few last minutes of their youth
As they pretend I am some kind of catch

For little do they know

And the few that did make it to the finish line
Ran away screaming in horror
At what lies behind these pretty blue eyes
And temporarily blond hair

Next!

The question is:
Will there ever be one
The one?
That I have waited for for so very long
That one, born of teenage dreams
Adolescent naivety, mixed with rock and roll
A few pints of good German beer
And a dream is born

All I ever wanted
To be a poet, expressing
My eternal, limitless love for you
To a waiting, wanting world

Yes, I am a poet (wannabe),
But expressing endless longing
Searching and abuse
In ugly, meaningless poetry
To a world that never did care
And has long since moved on
To sitcoms, fast food and pop stars

In spite of the ugliness of this world
I will continue

A heart, limitless
Infinitely cavernous
Loneliness is the echo
Of a single heart beating

Tip toeing around your feelings
I feel like a burglar
The dust of a strange household in my nose
As I smell your hair, a quick kiss stolen
Will I leave a trace on your heart
When you have moved on?

The winter drags, both outside and in
I search for the rare blossom willing
To defy the cold, mock the ice
Dare the elements of loneliness

To sow the seed of a happy spring

I long for your body
To feel your touch,
A brief moment of holding hands
Looking you in your blue/green/brown eyes
Perhaps falling in love just a little
Just let me find you, just once

                    Moonbeams,
Yes, the stuff of poetry it seems
And stars, shining so bright
Illuminate this clichéd night
As we sit on a stone
Contemplate, how we are alone
What I would do to have you love me
How you could give purpose to me
To feel happiness, just this one time
All I ask, it that you be mine
Then I may die in content, in love
And you are freed from these pointless words

Gruesome

Gruesome is the thought
Of what I will be going through
As I fly into the future and into the waiting
Arms of a death ready to surprise me
At any turn in the road
Ready to show me his true self, and all the pain
Agony and loss he is so willing to dish out
To us, the ragged living, the poor who
Were unlucky enough to conceive
Unlucky enough to have grown into a world
That knows death for what it is
Lucky are the unborn, and the animals too
Stupid to see his real face

And the dead, who have gotten it over with

I sit and wait for his coming, counting the seconds
That seem to go buy faster and faster
All the while I think of you,
What you could have been for me, a savior
A goddess that would envelope
And protect this poor spirit

It is not too late, don't let me fall
For I won't have the strength
To stand up again

Or look up, ever again…
I've seen the black side of life
        Lived on the blue side
                Glimpsed the red, sometimes
I want to live on a rainbow now
See it reflected in your beautiful eyes

I want to bathe in your color
Drown in art, love, music, poetry,
You
For all are one, and always have been

        Don't bother to execute me
I've been doing it to myself for years now
I know where to stick that knife
To cause the most pain
I know where to shoot
To let out the most blood
I know where that heart is weak
To cause the most loneliness
I know what words
Can cause the most bitterness
I know where the deformities lie

        I'm the expert at killing me
Not you!

I can lead myself to slaughter, thank you

                    Back on the scene
I advertise this pretty face
Put myself back on the market
Like I am selling toothpaste
And let the fat roll on in

Passion played by the actor I am
I lead you to the water, and you drink
You believe the lines I have memorized
And in my theatre, I play the same scenes
Over and over,
Tell the same stories
Over and over
Always for a different audience
And as the faces start to blur together
They all start to look the same
All that is left is you and I
Both of us, nameless

Yes, sometimes I do crave you
Your body, your smells, your voice
That look in your eye

As mean as your word, it could kill
Stabbing my fragile sensibilities
Viciousness projected, ejected, vomited

Into my gut, my tears hiding from your scorn
Your words had meaning, were mean

Ya know what I mean?

I am the crystal of ice
Floating aimlessly on an iceberg
On a desolate sea of tears
Even though the sun shines on me
It hasn't the strength to melt
The frozen, cold gloom

Forget art, music and literature
Fuck model trains, stamp collecting and football
My hobby is simply trying to understand
You

Rain
Pounding my senses, washing away happiness
Like the pollen, in clouds of yellow
Going down the sewers
On this gloomy, wet street

Rain
God cries, and we all feel his sorrow
His loneliness is contagious
He dooms us in our world
For his sins, not ours

Rain
Cleansing us of our dirt, accumulated
Guilt and regret
Then see the world anew
In all its splendid colour and sunshine

Fuck, fuck, fuck
Fucking is a synonym for life
Fucking is synonymous with life
Fucking creates life
Then life can get fucking hard
We spend our life trying to fuck
We spend our life thinking about fucking
We spend our life thinking about fucking someone
Else
We spend our life working a fucking job we hate
And finally, life fucks us over
And we fucking die

Wandering moods
Hold happiness captive
Push the spirit, against the wall
Bringing down the average
Of days happy

Woman, save your scorn for yourself
Where it belongs

I will continue to wander, without the guilt
You so try to inflict on this spirit

You may look, but not touch

This Bird Has Flown
Landed, eyed me suspiciously from the side
I made a sudden move, it took flight
Away from me, always away
I could never catch the bird

If I would start a new chapter
Will your name be the title?
Could your plot bring this story
To a happy end?

As a master
Manipulated
Form me into what you want, anything
That results in happiness
For you, for me, we

Us
Exists only in my passive vocabulary

I want to swim
Not in that pool of single, frustrated lovers
But in the beauty of your blue-green eyes

If I am in the middle of life
Why do I feel so dead?
I am tired of always betting
On the losing horse

    I am no longer the kicked dog
But the growling wolf, ready to spring
On your bones, to devour
A carnivore among helpless sheep
You are in mortal danger, my prey
And I, your predator, as I hunt for
Affection,
I become crazy, wild with hunger
At the faintest smell of your blood
Of you, coming near, coming to me
With me

In those long, dark hours, let us join our gloom
And we can hate the world together

But in the sunshine, our joy will blind the world
As we sing songs we always knew in our heart
But were afraid to sing

If you would only be my anchor
I could be your rock, and ready to roll!

My god, just give us a chance!

I sit here in the sun, doing nothing special
I think of you, and smile all day long
And feel like I have accomplished more
Than in all those years of gloom combined

I think I love you

> My heart is blooming
> Prettier and brighter
> Than my magnolia tree
> Outside my bedroom window
> On this beautiful, sunny spring day

The time we are given
For living, for loving
So unfair, so short

We all play our games, our daily rituals
Tricked into thinking, we are important
Our problems are unsolvable, our fears real
All the while our clocks are ticking
Relentlessly forward, because time
Doesn't give a damn about you
Me, or our love

Time is the ultimate, final enemy

Like a plane, high in the sky, flying with

The birds of song
We all must land, somehow
The only question is how

Loneliness is landing alone
Love is landing with your heart full of hope
Sitting next to the mirror or your soul

Your love could give me the energy
To conquer the world, to make it mine
Quality instead of quantity,
A few minutes of love
Compared to a lifetime of indifference
I found out the hard way

But perhaps, just maybe
It is not too late

I have surrendered this body
To many, as they gathered my seed
Collected my happiness, ripping
At my back as I performed

But none can compare to you…..

I am willing to let go and fall in love
If you are too
Willing to look like a fool
To you and the world

To bring you to laughter, to tears of happiness
To trust you, and be trusted
To be all that you want and ever dreamed of
If you do too

Pushing me into disgrace,
The laughter of the world
Bounces off the dreams
Of the true romantic
       Daydreaming like the stupid kid I am
I never grew up, never in my mind
Only in this withered, falling apart model
I was given without a choice

I daydream of a you that might not
Ever exist,
An ideal, not a benchmark
Of anything even remotely realistic

Show me who you really are, show me
So I can know
The passion, the intelligence
The beauty of reality
Your reality

       I step slowly outside my bubble of hope
Into a real world of cruelty, anger and indifference
Trying to find you before it is too late
Trying to save you before it is too late

Before you are swallowed by routine
Television advertising
And a nine to five job

Before this world grinds you down into
A conforming little wheel, feeding the chief
With your sweat and your effort
While he sits, fat and lazy
A turd on the pasture of mankind
He will never, can never know
The beauty of your spirit, the depth of your love
And understanding

He does not deserve you, never did

There are no groupies, never were
Never will be
Groupies fuck groups,
Not the lonely

This heart is true to you, whatever face
You may wear this day

Please,
Share your gloom
I know it all too well
It has been my only accomplice
Never to have left me

How about a dirty threesome, group sex?
Just you, me and our buddy gloom
Getting down to dirty business

Gloom is good at fucking

Hope
My holy grail of importance
Don't take it ever, away from me

Nurture hope, and it will bloom
Into a flower of color as you have never seen
Before

Nourish hope, and it can last a lifetime
A lifetime of hope, sounds good
Don't it?

Laid
You laid me, I laid you
Every artist knows
It isn't the quantity, but the quality
The form, the effect of gravity
And yes, even the color

You bring out the boner in me

The promise dawns
Finally finding the right road
Will I arrive on time?
All the paths are worn, devoid of bloom
As the lonely wander aimlessly

Honey bunny, my sweet honey
A taste of things to come?
How sweet life could be
If only you would wish to possess me
I would give myself to you

So I must catch myself,
The pendulum swings back to naiveté
As so often, ready to break me yet again
As I fear you have chosen gloom as your mate

For I have set my standards so damn high
That I am destined to be forever
Disappointed and lonely

Why bother to open the window
For
The sun has disappeared, yet again
I can hear the rain outside
I can hear the world crying
Its sadness invading me
Its sadness claiming me as one of its own

Sometimes it is all I can do
Just to keep even a speck of hope intact

I don't need to be religious
For I see hell all around me, encompassing me
Damning loneliness into my spirit
Damning me to grow old, alone

All I ever wanted, was someone at my side
Alas, another short chapter comes to an end
Expecting a long, grand finale
All I can offer are yet more bitter words
Of dashed hopes and perhaps
A few nice memories

Two Times One

As green eyes, me
Smile so bright, a gaze so lovely
Gentle words, and a love unfulfilled
Master the bitter, with hope so spilled

Although words so few, but a heart so big
Containing heaven, to cure the sick
As I fly to you in wonder
Must I wait, and take a number?

Let me sweep you off your feet
Let me love, and let me weep
Tears of joy, and of coming home
Never lonely, nor alone

But in the end, a joy so sweet
As you were never the one to meet
A kiss withheld, embrace was none
And so we parted, two times one

For Red Pepper, Blue

Red pepper, glowing blue
Eyes to water this bruised spirit
Golden long, curls sweep away
The blues of the perpetual winter

A promised hand leads to the promised land
Of a true kiss, a long embrace
A smile that tells of faith, perhaps love
That will defy our age, and endure
The indifference of those who wish us harm

For red pepper, whose glowing blue
Eyes, inquire and inspire, to lead and feel
Our way out of this jungle of hate

And into the world of hope, our combined
Freedom

Like music that touches the soul
As art that inspires the spirit
Love creates artists of us all
Transcending the borders of our age
Conquering the limits of our bodies
To be born again, immortal

As the battle is won, and the dust has settled
We view the world around us
With newborn eyes
We see the beauty within our reach
We feel the love within our grasp
All is as it should be
And should have always been
For we have come home to hope,
Peace and happiness